Let's Dance a Waltz

3

Natsumi Ando

Characters & Story

After an intense crash course in ballroom dancing, this chubby girl has transformed into a slim one!

Himé Makimura

Once a plain, ordinary middle school girl, thanks to ballroom dance, she has started to change. She achieved her dream of being partners with her crush, Tango, but she can't help worrying about his former partner...

Tango Minami

Himé's classmate and ballroom dance partner. He had given up on dancing for his own reasons, but Himé touches his heart and he enters the world of dancesport once more. He's very good at sports and popular in his class.

Former Partner

Let's Dance a Waltz

Himé always worried that she didn't live up to her princessly name. Then, something came along that gave her confidence: the romantic sport of competitive dance—a sport that requires a partner. Tango introduced her to this world, so she enters a competition with Yūsei in an attempt to bring Tango back into it. Her efforts touch Tango's heart, and at last the two become partners!

Their first competition as a couple is a big one, and they will be dancing against Sumiré and Yūsei. Tango almost loses his composure in the first round, but Himé's bright smile as she enjoys her dance brings him back to his senses, and the couple is showered with applause. And now, Sumiré and Yūsei have taken the floor. What will be the result of this competition? What about destined partners? This volume is overflowing with our four protagonists' love of ballroom dance!

Partners

Sumiré Shiraishi

A longtime friend of Tango's. She and Yūsei are currently the star couple of the Minami Dance School. She's a young beauty whose sophisticated charm makes it hard to believe she is only in middle school.

Yūsei Sudo

A longtime friend of Tango's. He and Sumiré are currently the star couple of the Minami Dance School. He's happy to be able to battle Tango on the dance floor again.

Contents

Chapter 9: Sumiré's Secret

YOUR SMILE COULD USE SOME WORK, SUMIRÉ-CHAN.
IN TODAY'S COMPETITION,
PLEASE LET ME SMILE LIKE A LOVELY VIOLET.
ぎゅっ
SQUEEZE
Let's Do Some Research, Part 1
All of the dance people that helped me with my research were very passionate!!
Even when I went to talk to a dance magazine editor...
That couple works really hard. I love their dancing.
Oh, yes, there are so many layers in the dresses. If you want to get some information on costumes, I can introduce you to some people.
Oh, and there's a competition coming up in XX city. When are you going to start dancing, Sensei?
Editor of a dance magazine.
How long have you been dancing, Editor-san?
He really does love dance.
Oh, I don't dance. Not at all.
Whaaat?!

POKE
POKE
NNRRNNGH
PFFT
TANGO, YŪSEI.
WHAT ARE YOU DOING? THAT'S SO WEIRD.
YOU LAUGHED!
DON'T WORRY, SUMIRÉ.
BELIEVE IN YOURSELF.
WE'RE RIGHT BEHIND YOU!!

WAAH
WE'RE WITH YOU.

WAAAH
...A—
AMAZING.

HUFF
SUMIRÉ-SAN REALLY IS TOTALLY AMAZING, MINAMI-KUN!
HUFF
SHE'S LIKE A SPARKLING WHITE SWAN!
HUFF
LIKE A FABULOUSLY DECORATED CAKE COVERED IN FRESH CREAM AND PILES OF FRUIT!
And... And...
DOWN, GIRL.
BUT...
HER DANCE IS JUST SO DIFFERENT FROM MINE...
WELL, SHE'S BEEN DOING IT SINCE SHE WAS FIVE, AND YOU'VE ONLY BEEN DOING IT SIX MONTHS.
SINCE SHE WAS FIVE?
SUMIRÉ'S PARENTS WERE STUDENTS AT MY FAMILY'S STUDIO.
THEY BROUGHT HER ALONG ONE TIME,
AND I GUESS SOMETHING HAPPENED THAT MADE HER WANT TO DANCE.
BUT I CAN'T GET HER TO TELL ME WHAT IT WAS.

BUT...
THE WAY SHE WAS DANCING TODAY...
GLOMP!
HIIIIMÉ-CHAN!!
LET ME GIVE YOU A CONGRAT-ULATORY KISS!
MMMWAH
WHAT ?!
HAVEN'T YOU GUYS SEEN IT YET?
THEY POSTED THE RE-SULTS.
SUMIRÉ-SAN?!
WHAT ?!
HUH ?!

WTSQ WTSQ WTSQ WTSQ WTSQ WTSQ WTSQ Total Rank Verdict
5 Sudō & Shiraishi 28 1 P
11 Tanaka & Inoue 6 8
Minami & Makimura 13 6 P
18 Abe & Sasano 2 12
1 Uehara & Sonoda 4 11
P...?
IT MEANS YOU'RE ONE OF THE SIX COUPLES GOING ON TO THE FINALS.
It stands for "pass".
!!
M-M-M-MINAMI-KU...N...
THAT'S WHAT HAPPENS WHEN I GET SERIOUS ABOUT DANCING.
WHAT DID YOU EXPECT?
F-F-F-FIN...
FINALS...
What... what a relief...
Wheeeew.

OOOH
OOOH
I CAN'T BELIEVE IT!
SO MANY CHECK MARKS!
YŪSEI-SAN AND SUMIRÉ-SAN GOT A HUNDRED PERCENT!
Shiraishi
& Inoue
Sonoda
SNAP
SNAP
LAST TIME, I DIDN'T EVEN GET *ONE!*
UH... THAT'S BE-CAUSE ...
THAT'S BECAUSE MY LEAD WAS BASED ON TANGO'S OLD ROUTINE.
SO YOU WERE BASICALLY DANCING WITH A MUCH YOUNGER TANGO.
THOSE WERE THE DAYS WHEN HE FLIPPED EVERY SKIRT HE CAME ACROSS...
AND HE COULDN'T GO TO THE BATHROOM AT NIGHT BECAUSE HE WAS AFRAID OF GHOSTS...
CUTE, LITTLE TANGO.
YŪSEI! YOU SECRETLY HAVE LIKE A MILLION GRUDGES AGAINST ME, DON'T YOU?!
BUT.
NOW, WE CAN DANCE ON THE SAME FLOOR AGAIN.
YES!
Yay!
ER...
HUH?

THE SAME FLOOR...?
...AS ALL OF THOSE AMAZING PEOPLE?
DRIIIP
だら
DRIIIP
だら
ぴゅ
ZOOM
I'M GOING TO GO BUY SOME WATER!
HUH? WHERE'S SUMIRÉ?
MAYBE I'LL RUN A LAP AROUND THE DANCE HALL.
I WANT TO KEEP MY MUSCLES LOOSE.
SHE WENT OVER THERE TO REST UP.
And cool down.
...

MURMUR
MURMUR
WASN'T SHE BEAUTIFUL?
SUMIRÉ SHIRAISHI.
SHE'S THE QUEEN OF DANCE, ALL RIGHT.
OH! BUT I LIKED THAT NUMBER 16 GIRL, TOO.
OH, HER!
SHE HAD SUCH A NICE SMILE.
IT WAS CONTAGIOUS. I COULDN'T HELP SMILING BACK.
I KNOW, RIGHT?
...
HER SMILE, HUH?

NO!
IT'S ALL WRONG!
IT DOESN'T MATTER HOW MUCH I PRACTICE.
I CAN NEVER GET IT.
I CAN NEVER GET THAT SMILE...

HEY.
IS IT FUN, HAVING A STARING CONTEST WITH YOURSELF?
T—
TANGO!
YOU DISAPPEARED.
I WONDERED WHAT WAS UP.
WHAT?
IS HE...
...WORRIED?
I WAS SURE YOU RAN AWAY 'CAUSE YOU WERE SCARED YOU WERE GONNA LOSE IN THE FINALS.

WHAT?
OH! THAT GIRL IN THE RED DRESS IS PRETTY CUTE.
Mrk.
AS IF YOU WEREN'T TERRIFIED THAT YOU WOULDN'T MAKE IT PAST THE PRELIMINARIES.
THAT FIVE-YEAR BREAK WAS HARDER ON YOU THAN YOU EXPECTED, I BET.
THOSE JUDGES WERE SOFT.
YEAH, MAYBE. I MEAN, THEY GAVE YOU A FULL SCORE, AFTER ALL.
BECAUSE I WAS PERFECT.
PERFECT? WHEN YOU DON'T EVEN NOTICE ME STICKING SIGNS ON YOUR BACK?
!!
I am the queen.
...
TAN-GOOO...
CUT THAT OUT!

BOP
コツ

LET'S SEE.

MINAMI-KUN WENT...

OH.

!!!

JUST A...
T... TANGO?
I DON'T THINK YOU HAVE A FEVER.
OF COURSE I DON'T!
DON'T DO THAT, IT'S CONFUSING!
CONFUS-ING?
HON-ESTLY.
WHAT? THERE'S SOMETHING IN MY HAIR.
Erk!
Gasp
WHAT DID YOU PUT ON ME NOW, TANGO?!

WHAT...?
JUST TELL ME YOU'RE NOT FEELING SO HOT, OKAY?
MAYBE YOU LOOKED NORMAL TO YŪSEI,
BUT THAT WAS CLEARLY NOT THE DANCING OF A HAPPY PERSON.
WHENEVER THAT HAPPENED WHEN YOU WERE LITTLE, YOU WOULD PUT THOSE IN YOUR HAIR, REMEMBER?

GOOD LUCK VIOLETS.

WELL...
I JUST HAPPENED TO SEE SOME AND PICKED 'EM THIS MORNING. THAT'S ALL.
AWW, MAN, IT WOULD'VE BEEN HILARIOUS IF YOU DIDN'T NOTICE UNTIL THE COMPETITION WAS OVER.
OH WELL.
AS LONG AS YOU'RE FEELING BETTER.
I WAS SURE HE'D NEVER NOTICE IF I WASN'T AT MY BEST.
16

HEY, TANGO.
REMEMBER WHAT YOU SAID TO ME BEFORE?
YOU SAID THERE ARE LOTS OF GOOD THINGS ABOUT MY DANCING THAT NOBODY CAN IMITATE.
WHAT KIND OF THINGS?
WHAT KIND OF...?
LOTS OF THINGS.
LOTS!

...
I THINK...
...YOUR DANCING...
...IS STRAIGHT-FORWARD AND POWER-FUL, JUST LIKE YOU.
STRAIGHT-FORWARD...
...AND POWER-FUL.
GASP

BUT HEY.
I THINK YŪSEI COULD ANSWER THAT QUESTION WAY BETTER THAN I CAN.
HE *IS* YOUR ALL-IMPORTANT PARTNER, AFTER ALL.
THAT PUNK. JUST HOW FAR DID HE RUN?
WAIT.
TANGO.
I...
I...

GRUMBLE
RUMBLE
RUMBLE
RUMBLE
MAKI-MURA?!
I- I'M SO SORRY!
SOMETHING INSIDE MY STOMACH...
UM
ER.
GYAAAAAHH!
I'M SO, SO STUPID!
WHY DID MY STOMACH HAVE TO GRUMBLE NOW OF ALL TIMES?!
PFFT!

Oooohhh!
HIMÉ-CHAN, YOU ARE TOO FUNNY!
Ah ha ha ha ha!
WHAT KIND OF PET WOULD YOU HAVE TO KEEP IN YOUR STOMACH FOR IT TO MAKE SUCH A LOUD NOISE?!
THE FINAL ROUND IS ABOUT TO BEGIN. WILL ALL DANCERS PLEASE COME TO THE DANCE FLOOR.
OH.
16
YOU TWO GO ON AHEAD.
I'LL WAIT HERE FOR YŪSEI.
LET'S GO, MAKIMURA.
I...
...THOUGHT SUMIRE-SAN AND YŪSEI-SAN WERE IN LOVE WITH EACH OTHER.
BUT... MAYBE...

MAYBE I'VE BEEN MAKING A BIG MISTAKE.
...
5
PATTER
パラ...

WE WILL NOW INTRODUCE THE COUPLES DANCING IN THE FINAL ROUND.
NUMBER 5,
NUMBER 16,
NUMBER 23
UM...
MINAMI-KUN...
THIS IS SO EXCITING!
DO YOU THINK SUMIRÉ-SAN...
THE FINALS.

Yeeeaaah!!
CONNECT MY FEELINGS WITH HIS.
THAT IS THE MOST IMPORTANT PART OF BALLROOM DANCE.
DON'T THINK ABOUT ANYTHING ELSE RIGHT NOW.
FOCUS ON THE DANCE.

ENJOY THE DANCE.
Whew...
5

I WONDER WHAT KIND OF DANCE WE'LL SEE FROM SUDŌ AND SHIRAISHI.

I CAN'T WAIT!

LET'S WIN, NO MATTER WHAT.

YŪSEI.

YEAH.

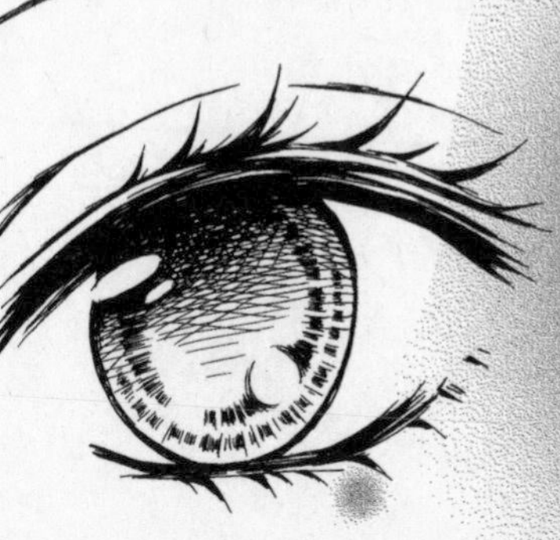

OOH
FWAH
I AM STRONG.
I LOVE DANCE, AND THE WAY IT HELPS ME EXPRESS MYSELF.
I'VE LOVED DANCING FOR MORE THAN TEN YEARS.
I CAN BE MYSELF THE MOST WHEN I DANCE.

IT'S WHAT'S MOST IMPORTANT TO ME.
16
NO, DON'T LOOK.
I'M NOT LOOKING.
I'M NOT LOOKING.

I'M NOT...
SUMIRÉ.
IF YOU'RE INTERESTED, YOU COULD TRY IT.
THAT...
THAT'S OKAY!
DOESN'T SUMIRÉ-CHAN WANT TO DANCE?
I GUESS SHE'S NOT INTERESTED.
SHE LIKES TO BE ALONE.
GLANCE ちら
GLANCE ちら
ぱっ FWUMP
Ah ha ha!
YOU'RE A LIAR.
YOU'VE BEEN SITTING THERE WATCHING THE WHOLE TIME.
AAAH!

WANNA DANCE?

YOU'RE
A LIAR.
Gasp

THE THING...
BUMP
...THAT'S REALLY...
...MOST IMPORTANT TO ME...
MURMUR

SUMIRÉ
...
Gasp

Chapter 10: Powerfully, Heartbreakingly

MURMUR
SUMIRE?!
SUMIRE-SAN?!

WHAT ..? WHAT'S WRONG?
SHE STOPPED DANCING...
MURMUR
MURMUR
WHAT DO I DO?
I...
...CAN'T MOVE.

GRASP

IT'S OKAY.
I CAN FIX IT.
CLAP
CLAP
CLAP

Huff
Huff
I WONDER WHAT HAPPENED TO SUMIRÉ SHIRAISHI.
MAYBE SHE TRIPPED?
DON'T SEE THAT EVERY DAY.
YOU DIDN'T TRIP...
...DID YOU, SUMIRÉ-SAN?
YOU WERE TRYING TO GET THAT FLOWER BEFORE IT FELL.
THE FLOWER MINAMI-KUN GAVE HER...
SUMIRÉ...
...

SUMIRÉ
HAS ME.
YEAH.
BUT...
TANGO.

OH, RIGHT.
IT'S BAD MANNERS TO TALK TO SOMEONE ELSE'S PARTNER IN THE MIDDLE OF A COMPETITION.

TAKE CARE OF HER, MAN.
I WILL.
AND NOW, ON TO THE TANGO.

SUMIRÉ -SAN!
CLAMP
WHAT ?!
H-HIMÉ-CHAN?!
HERE! PLEASE USE THESE!
WHAT ...?
IF YOU USE THESE TO KEEP THE FLOWERS IN PLACE, THEY WON'T FALL!

I KNEW IT.
SUMIRÉ-SAN IS IN LOVE WITH MINAMI-KUN.
JUST LIKE I AM...
IT WAS LOVE AT FIRST SIGHT!
BUT ...
WHAT ...?
WHEN I...
...SAW IT FOR THE FIRST TIME,
EVERYTHING SPARKLED IN FRONT OF ME. IT WAS LIKE, "WAAAH!" AND "NNNNNGH!"
And... and...
ANYWAY.

I'M IN LOVE WITH YOUR DANCING, SUMIRE-SAN!
NUMBER 16. PLEASE RETURN TO YOUR PARTNER.
I-I'M VERY SORRY !!!
Ha-wha?!
KONK
OWWW!
CHUCKLE
CHUCKLE

むにー

STUPID.

!!

STU ...?!

BUT...

...HE'S RIGHT.

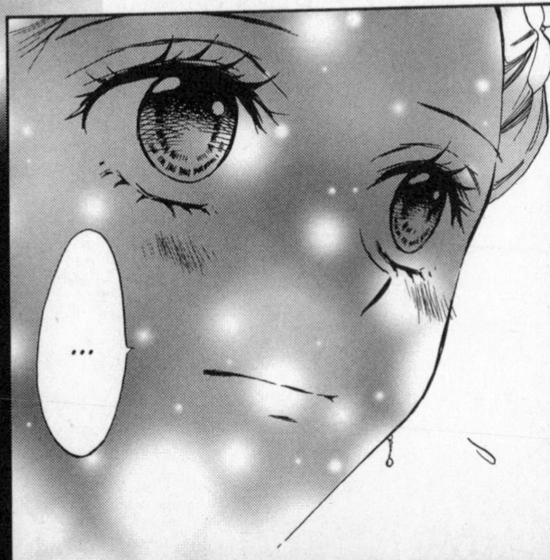

I'M EVEN MAKING HIMÉ-CHAN WORRY ABOUT ME. WHAT AM I DOING?

YOUR DANCING IS STRAIGHT-FORWARD AND POWERFUL.

SUMIRÉ...

THOSE FLOWERS...

NOW WE WILL BEGIN THE NEXT DANCE.

THE TANGO.

WHIP

SUMIRÉ-SAN.
WHOOSH

I FEEL THE WIND.
A POWERFUL GALE, RUSHING FROM ONE END OF THE FIELD-TO ANOTHER.
HIMÉ-CHAN IS KEEPING HER DANCE TOGETHER.
IF SHE CAN DO IT, WHY CAN'T I?

STOMP
I WILL DANCE.
A STRAIGHT-FORWARD, POWERFUL DANCE!!
SO AWE-SOME.

YOU DANCE 24 HOURS A DAY.
I JUST WONDERED WHY YOU LIKED IT SO MUCH.
HMMM.
WHAT DO I LIKE ABOUT DANCESPORT?
IF I HADN'T DISCOVERED DANCESPORT,
I THINK I WOULD STILL BE PLAYING ALL BY MYSELF.
DANCE CHANGED ME.
...MAYBE THAT I'M NOT ALONE.
SUMIRÉ.

THE THIRD CATEGORY, SLOW FOXTROT.
SUMIRÉ IS GETTING SERIOUS.
SO I NEED TO GET SERIOUS, TOO.
IF SUMIRÉ IS THE STAR,
THEN I WILL BE THE NIGHT SKY
THAT MAKES HER SHINE.
SHINE.
SHINE.

BRIGHTER AND MORE POWERFULLY THAN ANYONE.

OOH...
EVERYONE IS LOOKING AT SUMIRÉ-SAN AND YŪSEI-SAN.
IT'S LIKE THEY'RE THE ONLY COUPLE ON THE FLOOR.
5
JUST WHAT I'D EXPECT FROM OUR TOP DANCERS.
PERFECT BALANCE FROM THE TIPS OF THEIR FINGERS TO THE ENDS OF THEIR TOES.
NOT A SINGLE WASTED MOVEMENT.
IT'S LIKE WATCHING A BEAUTIFUL PAINTING.

WOW.
HOW IS SHE ABLE TO DANCE LIKE THAT?
SUMIRÉ-SAN'S STEPS...
...ARE MORE FLUID, WITH BIGGER STRIDES.
LIKE SHE'S STRETCHING HER LEGS OUT MORE...
SUMIRÉ-SAN REALLY IS AMAZING.
Mutter
Mutter
SHE HAS A BIG STRIDE.
Mutter
HER HEAD COMES OUT SO FAR.
HER SHOULDERS AREN'T SLOUCHED.
HER WAIST IS JUST TOO THIN.
Mutter
Mutter
IT'S LIKE HER BODY HAS... MORE TENSION?
IS SHE CHANTING?!
SHOONK
ACK!

IT'S NO USE.
MY LEGS
WON'T MOVE LIKE THAT.
CLAP
CLAP
CLAP
I HAVE SUCH A LONG WAY TO GO...
SIGH.
Huff
Huff
Wheeze
I'M STILL COMPLETELY TERRIBLE...
EEP!
KONK
NGH ...!
M- MINAMI-KUN?

MAKIMURA.
NONE OF THAT, YOU HEAR?!
YOU BETTER NOT BE THINKING ANYTHING STUPID LIKE
"I WISH I COULD DANCE LIKE SUMIRÉ"!
Huh?
HOW DID YOU KNOW?
HOW COULD I *NOT* KNOW?
I MEAN, THEY *ARE* AMAZING DANCERS.
BUT WE DIDN'T GET ON THIS DANCE FLOOR
SO WE COULD COPY SOMEBODY ELSE.
YOU ARE MY PARTNER.

AND I...
...LIKE THE WAY HIMÉ MAKIMURA DANCES.
THAT'S WHY I MADE THAT PROMISE, REMEMBER?
THAT I WOULD MAKE YOU THE MOST BEAUTIFUL DANCER ON THE FLOOR.

THE FINAL DANCE: THE QUICKSTEP.
WE ALWAYS START WANTING WHAT WE DON'T HAVE.
LOOK!
NUMBER 16.
BUT THE IMPORTANT THING...

...IS TO BE YOURSELF!!
NUMBER 16.
THEY'RE CATCHING MY EYE MORE THAN BEFORE.
HIS REFLEXES AND PIVOTS ARE STARTLINGLY FAST.
HE DANCES VERY ENERGETI-CALLY, MAKING GOOD USE OF THE FLOOR.
THEY'VE BEEN GROWING IN LEAPS AND BOUNDS THROUGHOUT THE COMPETITION.
THEY'RE SMALLER IN STATURE,
BUT THEY DON'T LOOK ANY DIF-FERENT THAN THE SUDŌ COUPLE.
HIS PARTNER RE-SPONDS WELL,
AND SHE'S HAV-ING SO MUCH FUN.
LIKE A BUD COMING INTO BLOOM.
16
5

FLOWERS!
DANCING FLOWERS!

DANCE-SPORT REALLY IS A MYSTERIOUS THING.
IT'S NOT LIKE I'M DANCING WITH HIME-CHAN.
BUT I CAN FEEL WHAT SHE'S FEELING.
AND SHE'S ...
...A STAR?

I DON'T KNOW WHY.
BUT I ALWAYS FIND MYSELF LOOKING AT ONE OF THOSE TWO COUPLES.

SNAP
カシャ
SNAP
カシャ
UNTIL NOW, SUDŌ AND SHIRAISHI ALWAYS DOMINATED THE JUNIOR COMPETITION.
Dance Club
WE HAVE SOME GOOD NEWCOMERS IN THIS COMPETITION.
THREE LIFELONG FRIENDS.
AND THE ONE LITTLE MOUSE WHO SNEAKED HER WAY IN.
パラ
THIS WILL MAKE FOR AN INTERESTING STORY.

Thank you very much for picking up Let's Dance a Waltz volume three!!

As for memories I have of when I was working on this volume, the main one would be that I got to go to Kokura and Hakata for autograph signings and workshops.

Volume

It was my third signing session in Hakata! Readers who had been reading my manga when they were in elementary school were all grown up! And for a second, I started thinking crazy things, like, "Have I gone through a time warp?!" But when you think about it, yeah....

It's incredible to meet readers like that. Here's to our miraculous encounters!

In Kokura, I went to the Kita-Kyushu Manga Museum. That place is amazing! It's paradise. You can read all the manga you want! And they have tons of manuscripts so valuable, I could have fainted at the thought of them. I don't know how many times I said "Whoa!" during my trip. I hope I can go again....

Chapter 11: His Old Partner

Let's Dance a Behind-the-Scenes Dance!
I love in dancesport when the leader does this (→) hand gesture, when he tugs on his sleeve. ♥ When I went to see my first competition, a lot of dancers were doing that before the music started, and it looked like they were preparing for battle, saying, "Okay, let's do this!" And I was all, "Is he saying, 'Just leave it to me!'? Eeeeeee!!"
Apparently, it's really just that their sleeves shift a lot, and they're fixing them.... But even after knowing that, I still get all excited to see them do it.

JAPAN'S TALLEST MOUNTAIN!
A LAKE AS BIG AS AN OCEAN!!
THIS IS GETTING EXCITING!
YES IT IS, MINAMI-KUN!

FROM DAD
ARE YOU IN YAMANASHI YET? GOOD LUCK AT DANCE CAMP. \(^O^)/
LOVE DAD
THAT'S RIGHT.
I'M IN YAMANASHI RIGHT NOW, DOING A TRAINING CAMP FOR BALLROOM DANCE.
AT THE COMPETITION THE OTHER DAY, MINAMI-KUN AND I ACTUALLY MADE IT TO FOURTH PLACE.
INCIDENTALLY, FIRST PLACE WENT TO YŪSEI-SAN AND SUMIRÉ-SAN.
A DANCE-SPORT ASSOCIATION HOLDS IT EVERY SUMMER.
AND WE WERE SELECTED TO PARTICIPATE!!

I CAN'T BELIEVE I GET TO COME HERE WITH MINAMI-KUN. IT'S LIKE A DREAM COME TRUE.
WE'LL BE TOGETHER MORNING, NOON, AND NIGHT.
Tee hee hee hee!
I FEEL LIKE I COULD REACH OUT AND TOUCH MT. FUJI.
COME ON, SUMIRÉ. LOOK OUTSIDE.
NO, THANK YOU.
I COME EVERY YEAR. I'M TIRED OF THE SCENERY.
BESIDES, AREN'T YOU FORGETTING SOMETHING IMPORTANT, TANGO?
HUH?
YOUR SUMMER HOME-WORK
IS TOTALLY BLANK.
Erk.

I'LL BE FINE. I HAVE A POWERFUL ALLY ON MY SIDE.
RIGHT, YŪSEI?!
ZNN
What?
SORRY, I WASN'T LISTENING.
HARSH.
YOU DON'T HAVE TO LISTEN TO HIM, YŪSEI.
SUMIRÉ-SAN...
SHE'S ACTING THE SAME AS ALWAYS.
SUMIRÉ-SAN...
...IS IN LOVE WITH MINAMI-KUN.

BUT MINAMI-KUN...
SHE WAS MY PARTNER—SHE WAS MORE IMPORTANT TO ME THAN ANYTHING.
...
...STILL CARES FOR HIS OLD PARTNER... EVEN AFTER ALL THIS TIME.
HOLD THAT POSE!!
AND DO SQUATS FOR TEN MINUTES!!

TREMBLE
ぷる
ONE MINUTE TO GO.
ONE HUNDRED SIT-UPS!
TREMBLE
ぷる
KEEP THOSE ARMS UP!
50-METER DASH! 50 TIMES!
BOX RACTICE* FOR 30 INUTES!!
GASP
WHEEZE
GASP
IT'S LIKE HYPER-CHARGED P.E.! I CAN'T TAKE IT!
FWUMP
ばっ
HERE, MAKIMURA. HAVE SOME WATER.

Wheeze
Wheeze
MINAMI-GUN...
IT'S YOUR VIRST DIME AT A DANZE CAMP, BUT YOU'RE KEEBING UP. THAT'S INCREBBLE.
ARE YOU OKAY?
FWAH
I GUESS YOU'RE NOT IN ANY SHAPE FOR COUPLE'S PRACTICE.
SUMIRÉ-SAN HASN'T EVEN BROKEN A SWEAT...
MAN, SUMIRÉ. SHE'S MOVING EVEN BETTER SINCE THAT LAST COMPETITION.

CLAMP
PLEASE PRACTICE WITH ME!
I HAVE TO GET BETTER! EVERY LITTLE BIT I CAN!
I DON'T WANT TO LOSE TO SUMIRÉ-SAN OR HIS OLD PARTNER.
AND RIGHT NOW,
THIS IS ALL I CAN DO.
I CAN'T JUST LIE AROUND DYING.
SNAP
SNAP

SNAP
パシャ
IT'S TRUE. ONCE YOU START DANCING, YOU GIVE OFF A WHOLE NEW AURA.
パシャ SNAP
?!
Wh-what?
WHO... WHO IS THAT...?
SORRY TO INTER-RUPT YOUR PRACTICE.
TANGO MINAMI-KUN AND HIMÉ MAKIMURA-CHAN, RIGHT?
WHAT ?!
A PIN-UP?!
!!

Dance Club
YES.
WE'RE DOING A FEATURE ON UP-AND-COMING JUNIOR COUPLES FOR OUR NEXT ISSUE.
A MAGAZINE FEATURE...
I'D LIKE TO GET AN INTERVIEW WITH THE FOUR OF YOU, IF THAT'S ALL RIGHT.
WELL, I DON'T MIND, BUT...
WOOOOW!
THEN I CAN DIE HAPPY!
パシャ SNAP
パシャ SNAP
ME, A PIN-UP MODEL!
NOT TOO LONG AGO, I WAS JUST MOUSE #4.
BALLROOM DANCE IS MAGICAL!!

UM...
IF WE COULD GET SOME MORE CANDID SHOTS...
Gasp
Aaaaaahhh!
I- I'M SO SORRY!
NOW, WILL YOU ANSWER SOME QUESTIONS FOR US?
SUDŌ-KUN AND SHIRAISHI-SAN.
AND MINAMI-KUN. YOU'VE ALL BEEN FRIENDS SINCE YOU WERE VERY YOUNG, YES?
AND YOU'VE ALL BEEN DANCING SINCE YOU WERE LITTLE? THAT'S REALLY REMARKABLE.
AND THIS LAST COMPETITION WAS YOUR FIRST ONE AFTER A LONG BREAK, WASN'T IT?
BUT YOU DANCED JUST AS WELL AS BEFORE. I WAS REALLY IMPRESSED.
WHAT ...?
OH, YOU SEE, I REMEMBER YOU FROM WHEN YOU WERE YOUNGER.

YOUR DANCING WAS AT LEAST AS DYNAMIC AS ANY ADULT'S.
YOUR WERE SO CHARISMATIC, YOUR PRESENCE DOMINATED THE FLOOR.
YOU WERE FAMOUS IN OUR EDITORIAL DEPARTMENT. EVERYONE TALKED ABOUT HOW YOU WERE GOING TO BE A STAR.
WOW...
MINAMI-KUN REALLY IS AMAZING.
AND YOU'VE BEEN TO THIS DANCE CAMP BEFORE, RIGHT?
HE'S...
...BEEN TO DANCE CAMP BEFORE?
BACK THEN, YOU WERE DANCING WITH ANOTHER PARTNER, RIGHT?
WHAT...?
I FOUND YOU IN AN OLD MAGAZINE.
TH-THAT'S OKAY. LET'S NOT TALK ABOUT THE PAST...
It's embar-

COME TO THINK OF IT, DANCERS CHANGE PARTNERS ALL THE TIME IN DANCE-SPORT.
I WONDER IF THEY COMPARE THEM.
LIKE, "IT WAS SO MUCH EASIER TO DANCE WITH HER"...
THAT'S ENOUGH ABOUT...
OH, HERE IT IS.
Club
はっ
BAH

IN DANCE-SPORT, WHEN YOU CHANGE PARTNERS, YOU CHANGE YOUR DANCING.
ACTUALLY, I GET EXCITED, WONDERING WHAT KIND OF A DANCE I CAN DO WITH THIS NEW PARTNER.
Oh, come on.
I NEVER DO THAT!
THAT'S RIGHT!
FOR ONE THING, TANGO WOULDN'T EVEN BE DANCING AGAIN
IF IT WEREN'T FOR HIMÉ-CHAN.
SHE *IS* HIS DESTINED PARTNER. SO THERE'S NO NEED TO COMPARE.
BESIDES, A DANCE PARTNER ISN'T LIKE A GIRLFRIEND OR BOYFRIEND.
IT DOESN'T GET THAT COMPLI-CATED.
OH, REALLY?
YES.
...

I DON'T KNOW.
IT'S IMPORTANT TO HAVE A STRONG BOND WITH YOUR PARTNER.
I DON'T THINK IT WOULD BE SO STRANGE
IF YOU START TO FEEL SOMETHING MORE.
WHAT'S THIS, SUDŌ-KUN? THAT'S A VERY SUGGESTIVE STATEMENT.
WOULD YOU CARE TO EXPAND ON THAT?
I'M SORRY. WE NEED TO GET BACK TO PRACTICE.
Oh...
CLATTER
WHAT A SHAME. I GUESS IT IS TIME YOU GOT BACK.

WELL, SHALL WE PICK UP WHERE WE LEFT OFF, SUMIRÉ?

Y-YES.

LET'S GO.

OH.

YES.

...

MINAMI-KUN.

I DIDN'T KNOW THIS WASN'T YOUR FIRST TIME HERE.

YEAH, WELL, IT WAS ONLY THE ONE TIME.

SO I'M ***PRACTICALLY*** HERE FOR MY FIRST TIME.

HIS MEMORY... WITH HIS OLD PARTNER?
ギュ…
I LIKE THE WAY HIMÉ MAKIMURA DANCES.

SINCE I MET MINAMI-KUN,
MY WORLD...
...HAS BEEN FULL OF SPARKLING JOY.
THAT'S WHY I GET SO SCARED.
IF HIS OLD PARTNER WERE TO REAPPEAR,
I'M AFRAID HE MIGHT LET GO OF MY HAND.
PLEASE, LET THINGS GO ON THIS WAY.
I'LL WORK HARDER. A LOT HARDER.
SO THAT ONE DAY I REALLY WILL BE HIS DESTINED PARTNER.

OOOH, THE STARS ARE SO PRETTY!
THEY'RE FILLING UP THE SKY!
THEY'RE EXACTLY THE WAY I REMEMBER THEM.

I BET IT BRINGS BACK MEMORIES FOR YOU, TOO, TANGO.
THE NIGHT SKY LOOKS LIKE THIS FROM ANY MOUNTAIN.
DID HE LOOK AT THE STARS WITH HER, TOO?
MINAMI-KUN... AND HIS OLD PARTNER.
...ERK.
SHAKE
SHAKE
YOU'RE LETTING IT BOTHER YOU TOO MUCH!
WHY DON'T WE GO OUTSIDE TO LOOK AT THEM?
WHAT?! NOW?!
IT WON'T BE A PROBLEM IF WE COME RIGHT BACK.
WE'LL ALL GO.
A WALK
UNDER THE STARS!
YOU LOOK HAPPY.
WHAT? WHY?
UM... JUST... BE-CAUSE.
I'LL BE RIGHT BEHIND YOU.
OH, YOU ALL GET STARTED WITHOUT ME.
YOU WILL? OKAY, WE'LL BE OUTSIDE.
I'll be right there!

OOOOH!
I FEEL LIKE THE STARS COULD RAIN DOWN ON US ANY MINUTE!
...
OH.
WHOA, THAT'S A BLAST FROM THE PAST.
I REMEMBER THIS HILL.
SO IT *IS* BRINGING BACK MEMORIES.
YEAH, I REMEMBER WE ALL SAT HERE TOGETHER, LOOKING UP AT THE STARS.

OH! A SHOOTING STAR.
BACK THEN,
TANGO MADE A WISH EVERY TIME HE SAW ONE.
WHAT? WHAT DID YOU WISH FOR?
LIKE I'D REMEMBER THAT.
I BET IT WAS SOME-THING STUPID LIKE, "I WISH MY HOME-WORK WOULD DISAPPEAR."
SHUT UP.
...I REMEMBER.
I KNOW WHAT TANGO WISHED FOR.

ZLRR
ZLRR
NNNGH...
I COULDN'T JUST *TELL* THEM I HAVE A POPPED BLISTER
AND IT HURTS SO MUCH I CAN'T WALK.
Why am I such a wreck after only one day of practice?
I WANT TO GET TO MY STARRY SKY DATE!
SOB SOB
YES. I UNDERSTAND. I'LL BE BACK BY TOMORROW.
WHAT...? I'M SORRY, YOU WERE FADING OUT.
HOLD ON. I'LL SEE IF I CAN FIND A PLACE WITH BETTER RECEPTION.
THE MAGAZINE EDITOR...?
RUSTLE
Tango Minami-kun (8)

THAT MAGA-ZINE...
I FOUND YOU IN AN OLD MAGAZINE.
BACK THEN, YOU WERE DANCING WITH ANOTHER PARTNER, RIGHT?
MAYBE...
IF I LOOK AT THAT... I'LL LEARN ABOUT HIS OLD PARTNER?
B-DMP
NO, NO!
MINAMI-KUN DIDN'T WANT ME TO SEE IT.
B-DMP
BUT...
B-DMP
B-DMP
B-DMP

I REMEMBER TANGO'S WISH,
LIKE HE MADE IT YESTERDAY.
YŪSEI?
FLIP
Tango Minami-kun's Partner
"I WISH..."

"...TO GO TO BLACKPOOL, WITH SUMIRE."

Minami-kun's
Sumiré Shiraishi-san (8)

Y... YŪSEI...!
I'M SORRY, TANGO.
I CAN'T LET EVERYTHING STAY IN LIMBO LIKE THIS.
IT'S HARD ON SUMIRÉ, TOO.
MY WISH...
...WAS THAT ONE DAY I COULD BE SUMIRÉ'S PARTNER.

BECAUSE I HAVE ALWAYS LOVED YOU, SUMIRÉ.

OH ...
YŪSEI...
UHHH.
I'M GONNA GO CHECK ON MAKIMURA.
PAT
ぽん
DON'T LOOK SO UPSET, SUMIRE.

THAT LAST COMPETITION, WE WON FIRST PLACE.
SEEING YOU THAT DAY, I MADE UP MY MIND.
JAPAN PASSPORT
IT'S YOUR PASSPORT. I ASKED YOUR MOM TO LET ME BRING IT.
I WANT TO GO TO ITALY, TO STUDY DANCE.
I WANT
TO AIM HIGHER.
WITH YOU.

NOT JUST AS A DANCE PARTNER.
I LOVE YOU FOR YOU, SUMIRÉ.
WHATEVER HAPPENS, I WILL ALWAYS BE BY YOUR SIDE.
I WANT YOU TO COME WITH ME.

MAKI-MURA...?
WHAT ARE YOU DOING SLUMPED ON THE FLOOR OVER THERE?
Tango Minami-kun's Partner
Sumire Shiraishi (8)
YOU...
WHERE DID...
...MINAMI-KUN?

MINAMI-KUN, ARE YOU
IN LOVE WITH SUMIRÉ-SAN?

Chapter 12: ...So Much

FIRST PLACE.
CLAP パチ
CLAP パチ
MINAMI AND SHIRAISHI.
CLAP パチ
WOW!
IT WAS SUCH AN ENERGETIC DANCE!
THEY BALANCED EACH OTHER PERFECTLY!
I CAN'T WAIT TO SEE THEM GROWN UP!!

SUMIRÉ-SAN
WAS YOUR OLD PARTNER, WASN'T SHE?
Let's Do Some Research, Part Three
Well? Have you?
Ha, ha, ha!
He's a god!!
Nice back-up! Thank you so much!
Aaahh!
No.
It'd just make things complicated.
A mature response!!
Oh...
But what about the girls?
So I asked some girls, too.
It's easy to ask girls.
PSST PSST
Hey, hey. Do you ever fall in love with your partner?
Never in a million years.
No way.
Ew.
They looked thoroughly disgusted.
Whoa.

YOU SAID YOU DIDN'T EVEN KNOW WHERE SHE WAS.
WHY... DID YOU HIDE IT FROM ME?
WHY...?
...
RUSTLE
IT HAPPENED AROUND THE TIME WE STARTED FIFTH GRADE.
PEOPLE STARTED TO LAUGH AT ME AND SUMIRÉ DANCING TOGETHER.

Hee hee
Hee hee
Hee hee
Hee hee
THAT COUPLE IS SO FUNNY!

BECAUSE OF YOUR HEIGHT...?
IN DANCESPORT, IDEALLY THE LEADER IS 10 CM* TALLER THAN HIS PARTNER.
BUT SUMIRÉ GREW FASTER THAN I DID.
WE COULDN'T EVER DANCE THE WAY I WANTED TO!
*ABOUT 4 INCHES
DON'T WORRY! WE CAN MAKE UP FOR THE HEIGHT DIFFERENCE WITH HOW GOOD OUR DANCING IS!
AT FIRST, I ACTED LIKE IT WASN'T A PROBLEM.
GULP
GULP
Milk
WHY WON'T I GROW?!
MINAMI AND SHIRAISHI, SIXTH PLACE.
OUR SCORES GOT LOWER AND LOWER...
THAT COUPLE JUST ISN'T REALLY *THERE* ANYMORE.

WE'LL TRY HARDER NEXT TIME, TANGO!
UH... YEAH.
SUMIRÉ SAID THAT EVERY TIME...
SUMIRÉ-CHAN.
ARE YOU WATCHING THAT AGAIN?
UH-HUH.
THE BLACKPOOL DANCE FESTIVAL!
I COULD WATCH IT A THOUSAND TIMES AND STILL BE AMAZED!!
LET'S DANCE AT BLACKPOOL WHEN WE GROW UP.
See? How they move there.
...

WHAT ...?
WHAT DID YOU SAY, TANGO?
I SAID I'M NOT GONNA BE IN THE NEXT COMPETITION.
IT'S NOT LIKE WE CAN GET FIRST PLACE ANYWAY.
THEY'LL JUST LAUGH AT US. IT'S EMBAR-RASSING.
BUT!
WE CAN DO IT! TO-GETHER!
COME ON.
BAH
JUST... ENTER WITH SOMEBODY ELSE!
TANGO!
IT'S BETTER THIS WAY.
IT'S BETTER FOR SUMIRÉ...
...TO DANCE WITH SOMEONE ELSE.

YOU'RE THE ONLY PARTNER FOR ME, TANGO!

YOU'D BETTER BE THERE!

I BELIEVE IN YOU!

BUT I DIDN'T GO...

BAM

THAT GIRL IS ALONE.

MURMUR

MURMUR

WHAT'S WRONG?

I BELIEVE IN YOU...
SHE WAS ALL ALONE ON THAT BIG DANCE FLOOR.
SUMIRÉ WAS TRAUMATIZED. SHE COULDN'T DANCE AFTER THAT, AND IT WAS ALL MY FAULT.
I CAN ONLY IMAGINE THE FEAR AND DESPAIR SHE FELT.

I...
TOOK SOMETHING FROM SUMIRÉ THAT WAS VERY IMPORTANT TO HER.
I SAW HOW HURT SHE WAS.
BUT I COULDN'T DO ANY-THING ABOUT IT.
BUT YŪSEI WORKED HIS TAIL OFF.
LITTLE BY LITTLE, HE MELTED HER HEART, AND BROUGHT HER BACK TO THE SUMIRÉ SHE USED TO BE.
IT WAS ALL THANKS TO HIM.
THANKS TO YŪSEI-SAN...

THAT'S WHEN I MADE A PROMISE WITH YŪSEI.
WE PROMISED EACH OTHER NEVER TO REMIND SUMIRÉ OF THE PAIN SHE FELT.
WE PROMISED WE WOULD PROTECT HER.
AND IT'S NOT ***YOUR*** FAULT ANY OF THAT HAPPENED.
BUT
THAT DOESN'T CHANGE THE FACT THAT I LIED TO YOU.
I'M REALLY SORRY.

IS SHE... STILL...
SPECIAL... TO YOU?
...
IT WAS ALL...
...ALL FOR SUMIRÉ-SAN.
I WANT SUMIRÉ TO BE THE HAPPIEST GIRL IN THE WORLD.

ぎゅ…
...OH.
I...
I THINK I FORGOT SOMETHING IN MY ROOM.
MAKI-MURA?!
THE GIRL MINAMI-KUN CARES ABOUT...
...WAS SUMIRE-SAN.
WHAT DO I DO?
WHAT...
...CAN I DO?

I'M REALLY SORRY.
—!
I WISH...
I WISH IT WERE ALL A DREAM.

WHEN I GET BACK TO MY ROOM...
...SUMIRÉ-SAN WILL BE THERE.
ガガガシャーン
CLATTER
CLATTER
CRASH
?!
S-SUMIRÉ-SAN?!
BAM
OH, HIMÉ-CHAN!
I JUST KNOCKED OVER THE TEACUPS...
Did I startle you?
O-OH, OKAY.
ER, THAT RAG YOU'RE USING!
NN?
AAAAAH! I NEED THAT FOR MY LESSONS!
CRASH
UMIRÉ-SAN!
CRASH

I'M SO SORRY, HIMÉ-CHAN.
Making such a mess out of things.
THAT'S ALL RIGHT. I DO IT ALL THE TIME.
RUSTLE
JAPAN PASSPORT
日本国旅券
A PASSPORT?
OH...
SUMIRÉ-SAN...
TANGO.
WELCOME BACK. YOU WERE OUT LATE.
YEAH.
I COVERED FOR YOU AT ROLL-CALL.
OH, THANKS. YOU COULD'VE GONE TO BED.

NO.
THERE'S SOMETHING I WANTED TO TELL YOU.
SHUT
パタン
HUH ...?
I DECIDED TO GO TO ITALY.
WITH SUMIRÉ.
ITALY?

YES.
TO STUDY DANCE. I'M GOING WITH YŪSEI.
GOING ...?
BUT, ARE YOU SURE?
YOU'LL BE SO FAR AWAY
FROM M...
...
FROM EVERY-ONE...
LIKE... YOUR FAMILY...
...BUT
IT'S WHAT YŪSEI WANTS.
SUMIRÉ-SAN?
SUMIRÉ.
SUMIRÉ, HE'S BACK AGAIN TODAY.

YŪSEI-KUN.

I KNOW YOU SAID YOU DON'T EVER WANT TO DANCE AGAIN.

BUT HE SAID HE'LL KEEP COMING UNTIL YOU CHANGE YOUR MIND.

HE SAID HE'LL WAIT AS LONG AS IT TAKES.

YŪSEI.
YOU SEE, I...
WHEN I TRY TO DANCE, MY FEET WON'T MOVE. I FREEZE UP.
DO YOU THINK I'LL EVER BE ABLE TO DANCE AGAIN?
YOU WILL.
JUST TAKE ONE STEP WITH YOUR RIGHT FOOT THIS WEEK, AND ONE STEP WITH YOUR LEFT FOOT NEXT WEEK.
I'LL BE WITH YOU EVERY STEP OF THE WAY. YOU'RE NOT ALONE.

IF IT WEREN'T FOR YŪSEI, I WOULDN'T BE WHO I AM NOW.
SUMIRE-SAN...
WHEN I'M WITH HIM, I CAN PUSH MYSELF HARDER.
SHE'S LEAVING MINAMI-KUN...
HIMÉ-CHAN?
GASP
I WANT TO THANK YOU, TOO, HIMÉ-CHAN.

I WAS REALLY HAPPY WHEN YOU TOOK UP DANCING.
I'VE ALWAYS WANTED A GIRL FRIEND MY AGE THAT I COULD TALK ABOUT BALLROOM DANCING WITH.
WHEN I TRY TO TALK ABOUT IT WITH MY FRIENDS AT SCHOOL, THEY ALL LOOK AT ME LIKE, "WHAT ARE YOU TALKING ABOUT?"
I KNOW. TAKE THIS HAIR ACCESSORY AS A THANK YOU GIFT.
TH... THANK YOU GIFT?
LET'S BE FRIENDS FOREVER, OKAY?

I'M...
...A HORRIBLE PERSON.
TO THINK THAT, EVEN FOR A SECOND...
...I WOULD WISH FOR SUMIRE-SAN TO DISAPPEAR.
SOB
ボロ
SOB
ボロ
WHAT ?!
HIMÉ-CHAN, NO! DON'T CRY!
IT'S NOT LIKE WE'LL NEVER SEE EACH OTHER AGAIN!
IT'S NOT THAT. I'M A TERRIBLE HUMAN BEING.
I'M THE SCUM OF THE EARTH.
—!

IT'S ALL...
...JUST TOO SAD FOR EVERYONE.
NO.
IT CAN'T BE THIS WAY.
BUT...
TODAY WE WOULD LIKE ALL THE DANCE CAMP PARTICIPANTS TO ASSEMBLE IN THE MAIN HALL IN THEIR DANCE COSTUMES.

IS THERE...
...ANYTHING I CAN DO?
I CAN'T WAIT!
WHO WILL I BE PAIRED WITH THIS YEAR?
?
HERE, MAKIMURA-SAN. DRAW A NAME.
A NAME?
What?
WE'RE NOT HAVING A LESSON?
TODAY WE'RE HAVING A SPECIAL EVENT!
DRAW A NAME, AND WHOEVER YOU GET IS YOUR DANCE PARTNER. ♡
IT'S NO FUN HAVING THE SAME OLD PRACTICE EVERY DAY.
I DIDN'T KNOW THEY HAD EVENTS LIKE THIS.
RUSTLE

OH...
...
WHAT ...
WHAT SHOULD WE DO?
WHAT ELSE CAN WE DO?
...
TANGO?
UGH. WHAT THE HECK.
Sigh
I WAS HOPING TO GET PAIRED WITH SOMEONE CUTE.
WHAT?
YOU WEREN'T SUPPOSED TO DRAW MY NAME, DUH. GET A CLUE.

Yūsei Sudō
I LOOK FORWARD TO DANCING WITH YOU, YŪSEI-SAN!
HIMÉ-CHAN.
SO I'M DANCING WITH YOU THIS YEAR.
IT'S BEEN A ONG TIME INCE WE ST DANCED OGETHER.
Y... YES, IT HAS...
I'M SORRY, YŪSEI-SAN.
Tango Minami

WHO DID YOU GET PAIRED WITH, SHIRAISHI-SAN?
Yūsei Sudō
YŪSEI.
Yūsei Sudō
THERE ARE ONLY TEN JUNIOR COUPLES. IT HAPPENS.
Sudō
ぱっ
BAH
THAT'S IT!
Yūsei Sudō
WHAT...? BUT... HIMÉ-CHAN?!
PLEASE.
TRADE WITH ME, SUMIRÉ-SAN!
THERE'S NO POINT UNLESS YOU DANCE WITH SOMEONE YOU DON'T ALWAYS DANCE WITH.

MRK
THAT'S MY LINE.
FOR ONE THING, NONE OF THE GIRLS HERE WANT TO DANCE WITH SOMEONE WHO HAS SUCH FILTHY MOTIVES.
YOU ARE SUCH A CHILD.
YOU COULD LEARN A THING OR TWO FROM YŪSEI.
I THINK YOU'RE THE CHILDISH ONE IF YOU CAN'T SEE MY CHARMS.

I JUST CANNOT TALK TO YOU, TANGO.
WELL THAT'S NOTHING NEW.
BUT THAT...
YOU TWO BACK THERE. WILL YOU BE DANCING OR WON'T YOU?
I'LL PASS, THANK YOU.
SAME.
WHY...?
—!

You big dummies !!!

WHY?!
WHY?!
WHY?!
M-MAKI-MURA?!
What the?
What's going on?
...
WHY...?
IF YOU TWO...
...ARE ACTING LIKE THAT...
I...
I...

NO.
DANCING WITH MINAMI-KUN IS SPECIAL.
YOU BETTER NOT FORGET IT!!
THAT'S SO YOU, MAKIMURA.
DON'T SAY IT...
I'LL MAKE YOU THE BELLE OF THE BALL.
I LIKE THE WAY HIME MAKIMURA DANCES.
—!

I...
...LOVE MINAMI-KUN, TOO.

I LOVE MINAMI-KUN.

MAKI-MURA.

SAYING IT WON'T CHANGE ANYTHING.

MINAMI-KUN'S HEART BELONGS TO SUMIRÉ-SAN.

BUT...

HIMÉ MAKIMURA,
LOVES YOU MORE THAN ANYONE, MINAMI-KUN.
Final Chapter: It Was You.

HIMÉ-
CHAN.

...
THOSE ARE MY REAL, HONEST FEELINGS.

NOW IT'S YOUR TURN.

MINAMI-KUN,
SUMIRÉ-SAN, YŪSEI-SAN.
YOU'RE ALL VERY DEAR TO ME.
YOU CAN'T GO OFF TO ANOTHER COUNTRY
WHEN ALL OF OUR FEELINGS ARE SO SCATTERED LIKE THIS.
Let's Talk About Noel
About once a month
I leave Noel at a pet hotel.
The pet hotel that he stays at will let me know how he's doing on their blog.
I wonder if he plays with the other
Noel-kun, lounging on the sofa.
A different day.
Noel-kun just
Another day still.
Noel-kun, on the sofa, watching over the other dogs as they play. "They're all in high spirits."
I've never seen a picture of Noel doing anything but sit on the sofa.

...
MY HONEST FEELINGS...
日本国
旅券
JAPAN
PASSPORT

RUSTLE
カサ
YŪSEI.
FSH
サッ
SO HIMÉ-CHAN CONFESSED HER FEELINGS TO TANGO.
THAT MUST HAVE TAKEN A LOT OF COURAGE.
YEAH.
...

AT THE COMPETITION FIVE YEARS AGO.

I...

...TOLD TANGO THAT I WOULD BE YOUR PARTNER.

WHAT ...?

TANGO DIDN'T KNOW WHAT TO DO.

AND I COULDN'T JUST SIT AND WATCH.

TANGO DIDN'T GO TO THE DANCE HALL BECAUSE HE THOUGHT I WOULD TAKE CARE OF IT.

IF WE REMIND SUMIRÉ OF THE PAIN SHE WENT THROUGH,
SHE MIGHT STOP BEING ABLE TO DANCE AGAIN.
LET'S KEEP EVERYTHING ABOUT THAT DAY BETWEEN YOU AND ME.
WHEN THE DAY COMES THAT YOU AND SUMIRÉ DANCE AT BLACKPOOL,
I'LL BE IN THE FRONT ROW, CHEERING YOU ON.
I WANT SUMIRÉ TO MAKE HER DREAM COME TRUE, NO MATTER WHAT.

—!
TANGO... SAID THAT?
I'M SORRY
IT TOOK ME THIS LONG TO TELL YOU.

I'LL GO TO ITALY BY MYSELF.
THINK ABOUT IT.
WHO IS REALLY THE MOST IMPORTANT TO YOU, SUMIRÉ?
YŪ...
...

CLACK
SUMIRÉ.
I DIDN'T KNOW THEY HAD A ROOM LIKE THIS.
TANGO.
I'M SORRY FOR CALLING YOU OUT SO EARLY IN THE MORNING.
YOU EVEN DRESSED UP LIKE I ASKED YOU TO.

MAY I HAVE THIS DANCE?

WHAT SHOULD WE DANCE?
LET'S DANCE A WALTZ.

SHOONK
ガ
OH!
WHOOPS.
I-I'M SORRY.
SORRY.

...
SUMIRÉ, I JUST...
TANGO, I JUST...
WH- WHAT...?
NOTH- ING...
Hee hee
Heh

DANCE REALLY IS INCREDIBLE.
YEAH.
I ALWAYS WANTED TO DANCE WITH YOU AGAIN, TANGO.
ONE DANCE TELLS YOU EVERYTHING.
...
ME, TOO.

MINAMI-KUN AND SUMIRE-SAN...
THEY GOT THROUGH TO EACH OTHER.
I'M HAPPY FOR THEM.
I... REALLY AM...
GNN
...

YEAH!
HIMÉ-CHAN.
ARE YOU SURE YOU WANT TO GO HOME EARLY?!
OH...
THANK YOU, HIMÉ-CHAN.
YES! I HAVE SOME THINGS TO TAKE CARE OF. THANK YOU VERY MUCH!
...

GOODBYE...

MINAMI-KUN.

MMMM!

UMEBOSHI IS THE ONLY THING TO PUT ON A STEAMING BOWL OF RICE! ♪

HIMÉ.

YOU'VE SURE BEEN EATING A LOT SINCE YOU GOT BACK FROM CAMP.

YEAH. KEEPING UP YOUR STRENGTH IS ONE OF THE BASICS OF DANCE!
AND I'M MEETING MY NEW PARTNER TODAY.
I put a want ad in a magazine.
I HAVE TO KEEP MOVING FORWARD.
SO THAT THE NEXT TIME I SEE MINAMI-KUN, I CAN GREET HIM WITH A SMILE.
HI.
I FEEL SO LUCKY TO PAIR UP WITH A VETERAN DANCER.
I LOOK FORWARD TO DANCING TOGETHER, TOO.
NOW LET'S GET STARTED!
WHAT? ALREADY?
WOW.
YOU MUST REALLY LIKE DANCING.
I DO!
BECAUSE DANCE IS WHAT HELPED ME...
...CHANGE FROM BEING A MOUSE.

UH...
HUH...?
YOU'RE VERY EASY TO DANCE WITH.
THANK YOU,
MINA...

NO...
BECAUSE DANCE IS WHAT...
NO, THAT'S NOT TRUE.
MINAMI-KUN IS WHAT HELPED ME.
THE REASON I CHANGED,
THE REASON I HAD SO MUCH FUN DANCING.
IT WAS ALL...
ALL BECAUSE MINAMI-KUN...
...WAS THE ONE HOLDING MY HAND.

MINAMI-KUN.
I'M SO STUPID.
HUH? WHAT'S WRONG?
I CAN'T EVER FORGET HIM.
MINAMI-KUN...

HEY.
I THOUGHT I TOLD YOU, YOU CAN'T DANCE IF YOU'RE LOOKING DOWN.

MI...
MINAMI-K...
HUH...? I THOUGHT YOU DIDN'T HAVE A PARTNER.
IT... IT CAN'T BE...
MINAMI-KUN?
WHY...?
I... I MEAN...
WHAT ABOUT SUMIRÉ-SAN?

SUMIRÉ-SAN IS YOUR DESTINED PARTNER, ISN'T SHE?
I MEAN, YOU WERE DANCING SO WONDERFULLY TOGETHER...
OH.
YOU SAW THAT?
SUMIRÉ AND I AREN'T DESTINED PARTNERS.
WHEN I DANCED WITH HER, I COULD TELL.
SHE'S GOTTEN REALLY GOOD.
HER HOLDS,
HER FOOT-WORK...
YŪSEI WAS IN ALL OF IT.

YŪSEI IS SUMIRÉ'S BEST PARTNER.
AND I THINK SHE REALIZES THAT, TOO.
WHAT ...?
WHAT I REALLY LOVED
WAS DANCING WITH *YOU*.
SUMIRÉ... WHAT DID YOU SAY?

I WANT TO BE WITH YOU, YŪSEI.
BUT MAYBE I'M JUST SAYING WHAT I THINK YOU WANT TO HEAR.
I'VE WAITED
A LONG TIME TO HEAR YOU SAY THAT.

SUMIRÉ-SAN...
I'M HAPPY FOR HER.
AFTER THAT COMPETITION,
I ASSUMED THAT THE HANDS OF HER CLOCK HAD STOPPED MOVING.
BUT THEY NEVER STOPPED. SHE WAS ALWAYS MOVING FORWARD.
AND I REALIZED...
...WHAT I'VE BEEN LOOKING FOR.
SFF
TO BE HONEST, I CAN'T SEE YOU AS ANYTHING MORE THAN A DANCE PARTNER.
BUT RIGHT NOW,
YOU'RE THE ONLY ONE I WANT TO DANCE WITH.

HIMÉ.

...R
REAL
...
...
LY?
DO
YOU...
MEAN
IT...?
HIME.

NNNNGH!
HEY, YOU DON'T NEED TO CRY *THAT* MUCH.
I MEAN IT.
BUT...
YOU CALLED ME HIMÉ.
THAT'S MY FIRST NAME.
AND HIMÉ...
... MEANS PRIN-CESS.
I NEVER HAD ANY CONFIDENCE IN IT BEFORE.
BUT JUST HEARING IT FROM MINAMI-KUN'S MOUTH MAKES IT FEEL SO SPECIAL.
SQUEEZE
I AM YOUR DESTINED PARTNER, MINAMI-KUN. I KNOW I AM!

I LOVE YOU!
B-DMP
OH? MINAMI-KUN, YOUR FACE IS RED.
Y-YOU'RE IMAGINING IT.
PLEASE CALL ME HIMÉ AGAIN.
D-DON'T PUSH IT!

BLACKPOOL.
A FEW YEARS LATER.
SOMEONE ONCE SAID
SEE? I TOLD YOU.
WHEN YOU MEET YOUR IDEAL PARTNER, YOU KNOW THE INSTANT YOU TAKE HER HAND.
YEAH.

YOU WERE MY DESTINED PARTNER.
MY PRINCESS.
AS IF...
...YOU WERE DESTINED TO BE TOGETHER.
★★ The End ★★

Special Thanks!!

Nakamura-sama
Miyaji-sama
Ueno-sama
Nakayama-sama

The Nakayoshi editorial department
Yonemura-sama, Hino-sama
M's Dance Academy
Wakashira-sensei, Tatsumi-sensei
Kawatami Design-sama

Let's Talk to Papa

A Kodansha Comics Trade Paperback Original.

Published in the United States by Kodansha Comics, an imprint of Kodansha USA Publishing, LLC, New York.

Publication rights for this English edition arranged through Kodansha Ltd., Tokyo.

First published in Japan in 2014 by Kodansha Ltd., Tokyo as *Waltz no Ojikan*, volume 3.

ISBN 978-1-63236-048-9

Printed in the United States of America.

www.kodanshacomics.com

9 8 7 6 5 4 3 2 1

Translator: Alethea Nibley & Athena Nibley
Lettering: Jennifer Skarupa